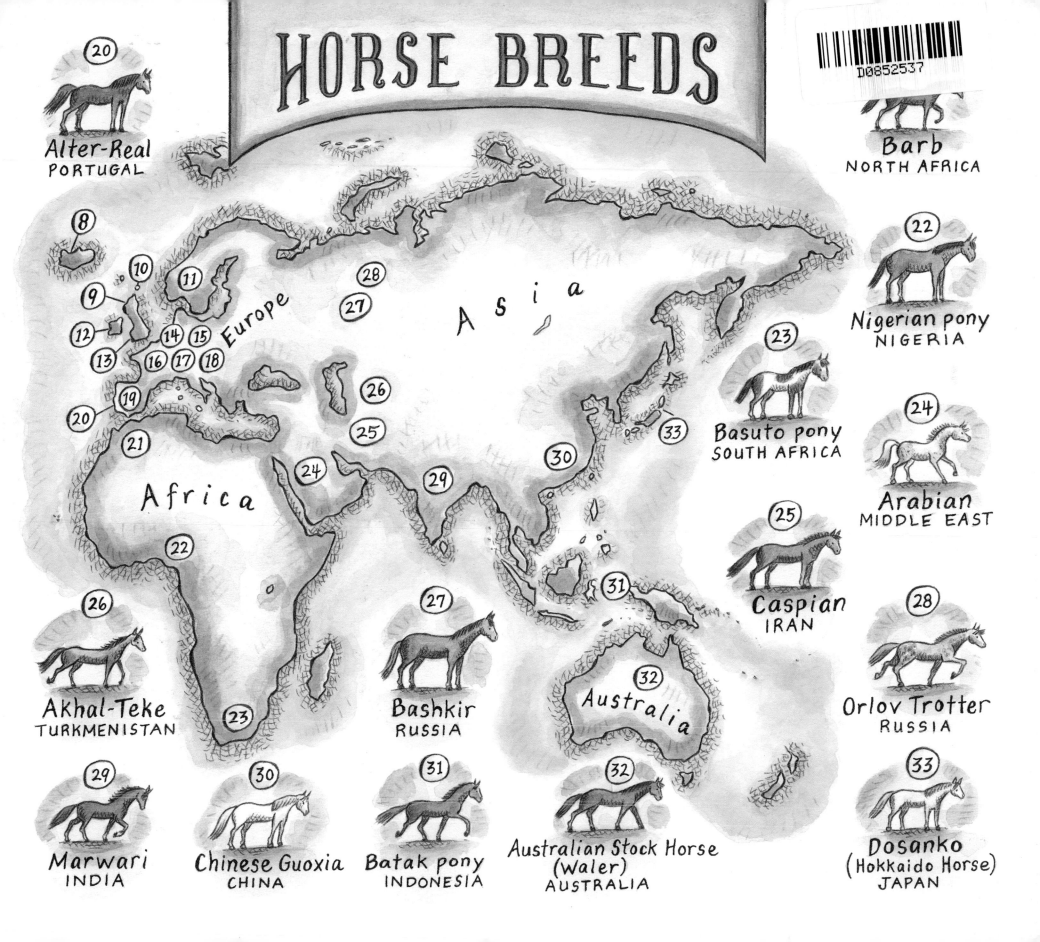

# HORSE BREEDS

20 Alter-Real PORTUGAL

Barb NORTH AFRICA

22 Nigerian pony NIGERIA

23 Basuto pony SOUTH AFRICA

24 Arabian MIDDLE EAST

25 Caspian IRAN

26 Akhal-Teke TURKMENISTAN

27 Bashkir RUSSIA

28 Orlov Trotter RUSSIA

29 Marwari INDIA

30 Chinese Guoxia CHINA

31 Batak pony INDONESIA

32 Australian Stock Horse (Waler) AUSTRALIA

33 Dosanko (Hokkaido Horse) JAPAN

Europe

Asia

Africa

Australia

# HORSE POWER

## HOW HORSES CHANGED THE WORLD

JENNIFER THERMES

Abrams Books for Young Readers · New York

Parahippus

Pliohippus

Equus
The modern horse~
4 million years ago

Miohippus

Dinohippus

Kalobatippus

Merychippus

Hipparion

Epihippus

Mesohippus

Orohippus

Eohippus,
Hyracotherium, or
"dawn horse"~
56 million years ago

Horses belong to the Equidae family, which includes donkeys and zebras. They are also distant relatives of the tapir and the rhinoceros!

About fifty-six million years ago, horses first appeared on earth. The earliest-known ancestors of the modern horse lived in North America. The size of dogs, with toes on their feet, they nibbled tender leafy plants that grew from the warm, steamy earth. They fled from dire wolves, saber-toothed tigers, and other hungry predators who might eat them.

The eons passed and earth slowly cooled. Jungles turned to grassland. Some branches of the horse family evolved and survived to become bigger and faster, with single hooves and strong teeth. Others did not.

And then, eleven thousand years ago, horses disappeared from the continent. Perhaps it was a sudden natural disaster or the effects of a changing climate. No one knows for sure.

But through the ages, a few horses had followed the grassy plains that once connected North America to Asia. They spread far and wide. Horses prevailed!

Across Eurasia, prehistoric humans roamed from place to place, hunting horses for food, and drawing images of horses on walls deep inside dark caves. When humans finally settled on the land, they planted crops and raised goats, sheep, chickens, oxen, and then horses—for meat and milk. Horses were one of the last species to be domesticated.

About six thousand years ago, when horses first let humans climb astride their backs, a world of change was set in motion.

The first wheel was invented 5,500 years ago in Mesopotamia for pottery making. Wheels would transform transportation.

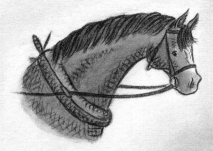

The horse collar allowed a horse to pull heavy loads without choking its windpipe. It was invented in China and later spread to Europe.

Saddles, stirrups, bits, and bridles helped a rider to stay on a horse's back and have better control of the animal.

Iceland

NORTH SEA

Scandinavia

EUROPE

ATLANTIC OCEAN

Eurasia

CASPIAN SEA

BLACK SEA

MEDITERRANEAN SEA

Mesopotamia

PERSIAN GULF

North Africa

A F R I C A

RED SEA

Arabian Peninsula

ARABIAN SEA

Map shows horses through time and modern-day borders!

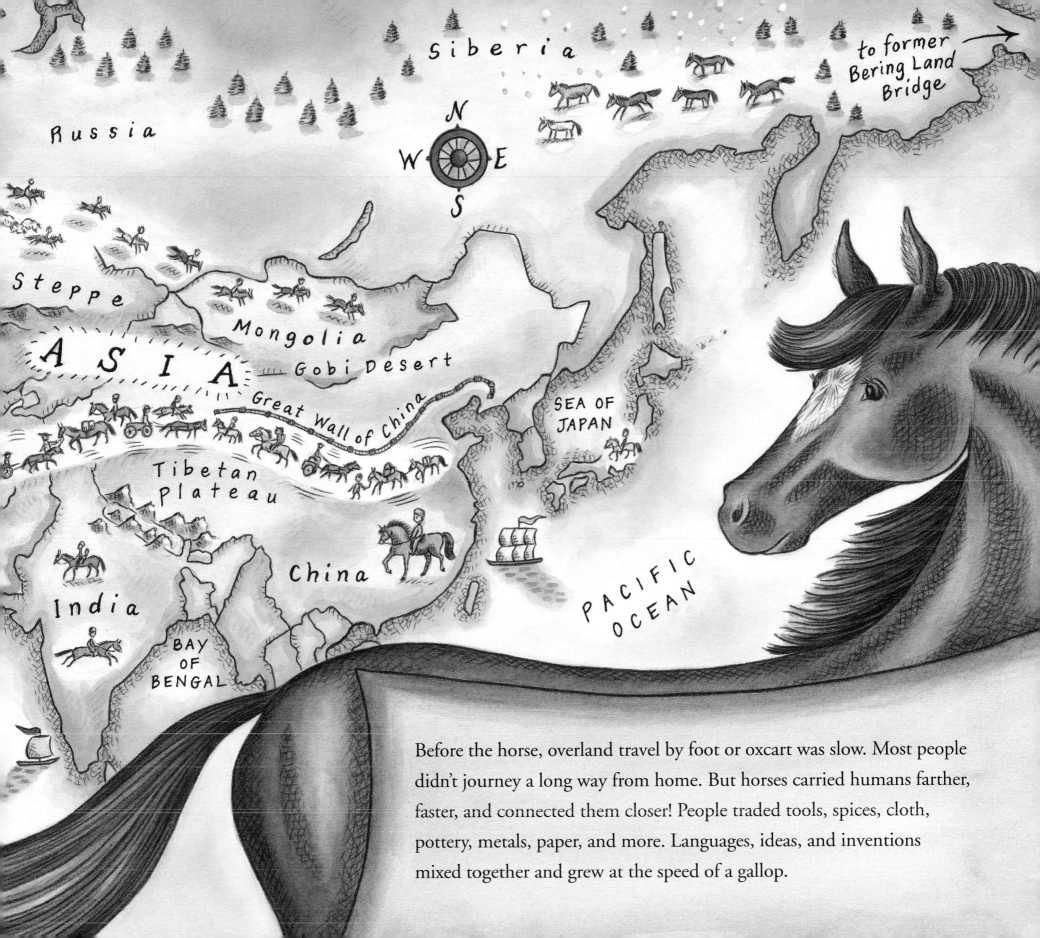

Siberia

to former Bering Land Bridge

Russia

N
W · E
S

Steppe

ASIA

Mongolia

Gobi Desert

Great Wall of China

Tibetan Plateau

SEA OF JAPAN

China

PACIFIC OCEAN

India

BAY OF BENGAL

Before the horse, overland travel by foot or oxcart was slow. Most people didn't journey a long way from home. But horses carried humans farther, faster, and connected them closer! People traded tools, spices, cloth, pottery, metals, paper, and more. Languages, ideas, and inventions mixed together and grew at the speed of a gallop.

Horses are herd animals, which helps to keep them safe. They form social bonds with other horses and animals—including humans! This is one reason they were easier to domesticate.

A horse's coat protects it from the elements—from short and sleek to keep it cool in hot climates, to long and shaggy for warmth in cold, wet weathe

A long tail comes in handy to swipe pesky flies away!

Some horse types:

pony

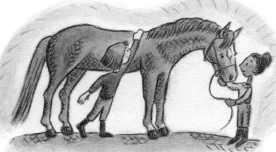

light saddle horse

heavy draft horse

Horses have special ligaments that stabilize their joints so they can doze while standing, and dash away quickly if they need to!

Horses evolved to graze on small amounts of food throughout the day. Food is digested quickly so that a horse can literally eat and run (unlike cows or oxen).

# HORSE SO SPECIAL?

he horse's long back is strong enough carry humans and other weight.

A horse's height is measured in "hands" to the top of its withers. One hand equals four inches.

Ears rotate individually to hear approaching predators, and express a horse's mood.

Eyes placed high on the sides of a horse's head mean that it can watch for danger when its head is lowered to graze. Horses can see in almost all directions except for directly behind and directly in front.

A horse's teeth become worn down from eating tough grasses, so they grow throughout its entire life. They are also a good way to estimate a horse's age. The gap in a horse's teeth, called the "diastema," makes a perfect spot for a bridle's bit.

The muzzle includes a horse's nostrils, chin, and sensitive mouth. A clever horse can open a door latch with its lips!

A big chest and lungs mean that a horse can inhale large amounts of oxygen and run for long stretches of time.

Hard, single-toed hooves help a horse run swiftly over different terrain. A horse can use its hooves to paw through snow and reach pasture in the winter to avoid starvation.

The horse evolved with traits that helped it survive when other species became extinct. It could live in many different environments around the world, and it was made to run!

Many cultures have used the horse throughout history. Vikings from Scandinavia invaded new lands by sea. They brought small, sturdy horses to places like Iceland. These horses have barely changed in more than one thousand years.

Kingdoms in Europe used large, heavy horses that could charge powerfully in battle or could bear the weight of a knight's armor in jousting tournaments. Horses were a symbol of status and wealth.

Swift, light horses that were tolerant of the heat and had little need for water transported nomadic desert tribes across the Arabian Peninsula and North Africa, into what is known today as Spain.

Strong, shaggy mounts carried people of Central Asia for miles across the frozen tundra as they migrated with their herds of sheep and other animals through the seasons.

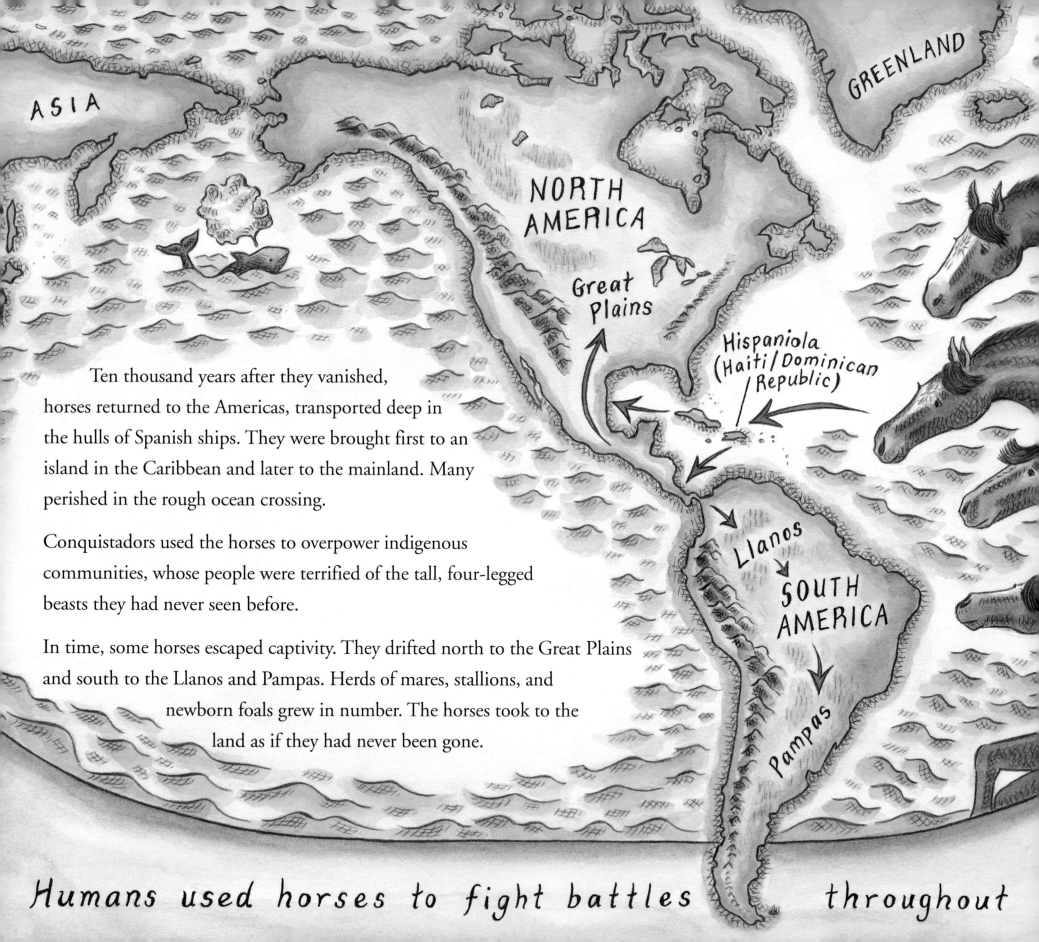

ASIA

GREENLAND

NORTH AMERICA

Great Plains

Hispaniola (Haiti / Dominican Republic)

SOUTH AMERICA

Llanos

Pampas

Ten thousand years after they vanished, horses returned to the Americas, transported deep in the hulls of Spanish ships. They were brought first to an island in the Caribbean and later to the mainland. Many perished in the rough ocean crossing.

Conquistadors used the horses to overpower indigenous communities, whose people were terrified of the tall, four-legged beasts they had never seen before.

In time, some horses escaped captivity. They drifted north to the Great Plains and south to the Llanos and Pampas. Herds of mares, stallions, and newborn foals grew in number. The horses took to the land as if they had never been gone.

Humans used horses to fight battles throughout

history. Horses never chose to go to war.

Before horses, Native people across the Great Plains of North America used dogs and travois sleds to pull heavy loads and move their camps from place to place. They hunted bison on foot. But once they had horses of their own, Native Americans became master riders. Horses made life easier! This era lasted just two hundred years.

In that time, Native Americans would be forced off the land they had lived on for millennia, and onto reservations.

Horses, mules, and oxen pulled covered wagons westward through rivers, across prairies, and over mountain ranges, where European settlers claimed the vast continent as their own.

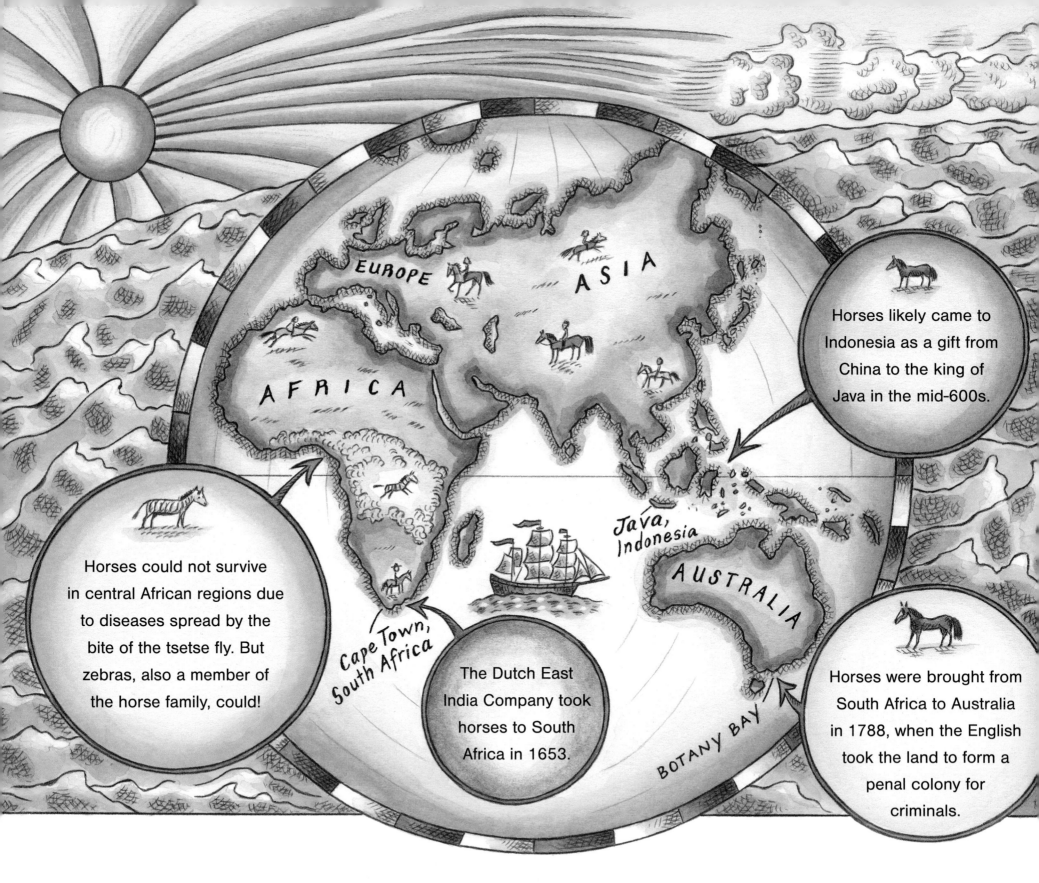

Horses likely came to Indonesia as a gift from China to the king of Java in the mid-600s.

Horses could not survive in central African regions due to diseases spread by the bite of the tsetse fly. But zebras, also a member of the horse family, could!

The Dutch East India Company took horses to South Africa in 1653.

Horses were brought from South Africa to Australia in 1788, when the English took the land to form a penal colony for criminals.

EUROPE

ASIA

AFRICA

Java, Indonesia

AUSTRALIA

Cape Town, South Africa

BOTANY BAY

Wherever humans ventured around the globe, horses were by their side.

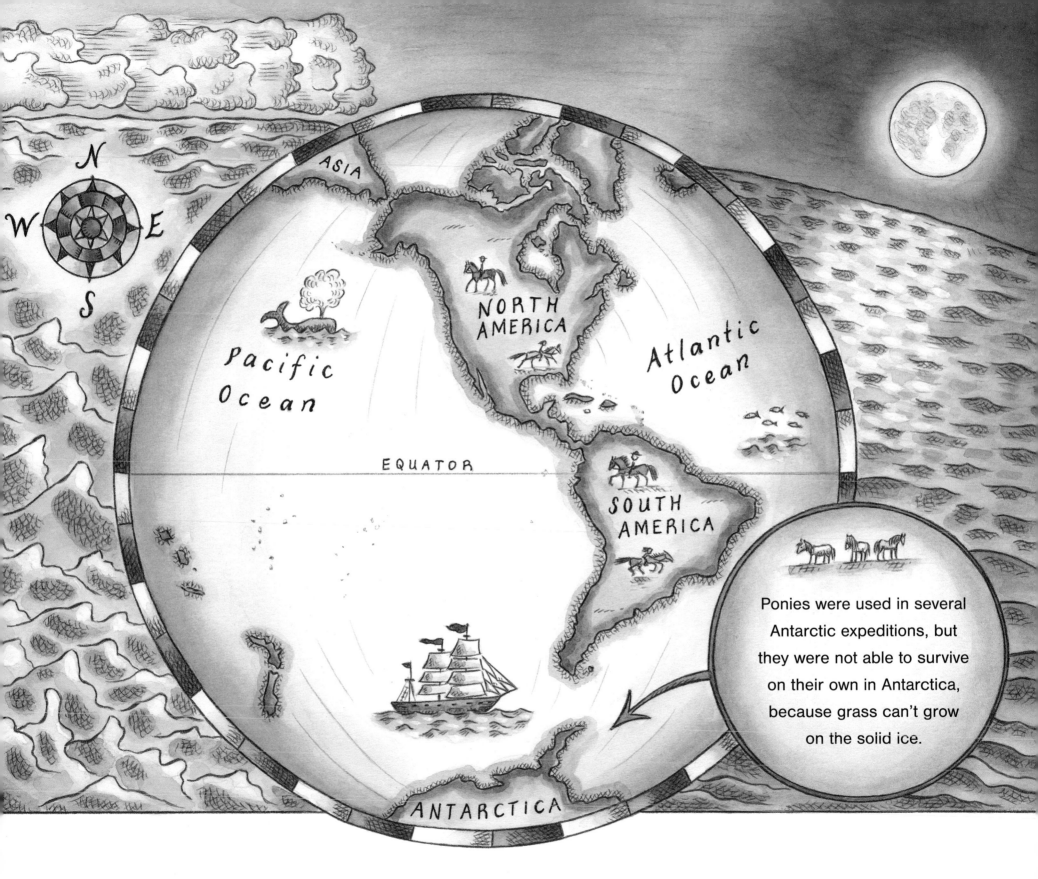

Ponies were used in several Antarctic expeditions, but they were not able to survive on their own in Antarctica, because grass can't grow on the solid ice.

By the late eighteenth century, horses lived on every continent except for Antarctica!

Before telephones, cell phones, and the internet, horses enabled humans to communicate.

From teams of horses and riders relaying messages across ancient Persia,

throughout the Roman Empire's postal system with fifty thousand miles of roads,

to regularly scheduled mail delivery in England—humans kept in contact, thanks to the horse!

For just under two years, the Pony Express sped across two thousand miles of the western United States to deliver letters and small packages. When the transcontinental telegraph line connected the East and West Coasts, news could be sent faster via electrical signals.

In time, humans created inventions to help them farm more land and grow more crops. Horses powered steel plows, seeders, harrowers, mowers, and reapers. Horses pulled the wagons that delivered the harvest to market.

From when they were first tamed, horses were bred by humans for specific traits and uses. Many new breeds were created in the last few centuries, including giant draft horses, smooth-gaited saddle horses, high-stepping hackney ponies, and speedy racehorses—because humans have always loved to watch horses run.

All Thoroughbred racehorses are descendants of three original stallions!

THE BYERLEY TURK          THE GODOLPHIN BARB          THE DARLEY ARABIAN

Electricity, machines, and steam-powered engines transformed the world during the Industrial Revolution. But horses were not cast aside. Horses moved the goods that were manufactured in big factories. They hauled the coal that fueled new steam locomotives, known as "iron horses." *And* they transported people where train tracks didn't go.

Horses were needed more than ever.

"Horsepower" is a unit of measurement that originally compared the power of a steam engine to the power of a horse. It is defined in different ways depending on the type of power, and the term is still in use today!

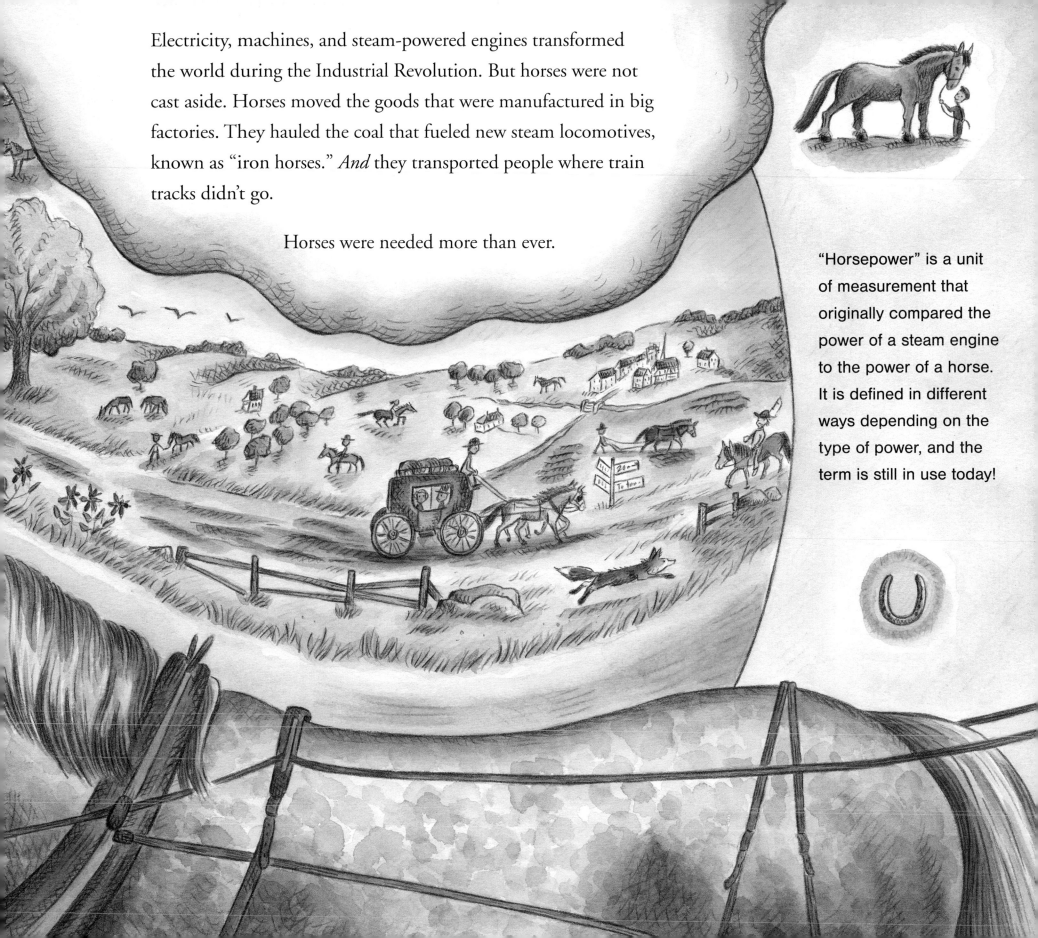

One horse produces an average of 35 pounds of manure daily. In 1900, more than 130,000 horses lived in New York City, which meant millions of pounds of fresh "road apples" in the streets every day!

City horses were trained to stay calm through the noise and frenzy of a big metropolis. Some wore blinkers to shield their eyes from sudden movements, since their natural instinct is to run when frightened. Without horses, human society would have been brought to a halt.

Horses were the engines that powered *everything*.

# HORSES POWER

Pack horses

Delivery horses (for eggs, meat, cheese, milk, and other food)

Street-sweeper horses (to clear manure from streets)

Ambulance horses

Canal barge-pulling horses

Carriage

Ice-delivery horses (to keep food cold)

Police horses

Fire-engine horses

Because of horses, there were jobs for humans! Leather tanners, harness makers, saddlers, ironworkers (to forge iron), blacksmiths (to make millions of iron horseshoes and horseshoe nails), farriers (to put the shoes *on* the horses),

# ED THE WORLD!

Timber-hauling horses

Farm horses

Ranch horses

Horse car and omnibus horses

horses

Construction horses

Cab horses

Coal-mine pit ponies
(for heat and to power
steam engines)

"Night soil" horses
(to remove human excrement!)

wheelwrights, carriage builders, farmers (to grow hay and grain to feed the horses), feed merchants, stablehands, grooms, teamsters (horse drivers), veterinarians, and more . . .

And then came the car.

The first automobiles were invented in the late 1800s. They were powered by gasoline engines and speedier than a horse! People were smitten with the newfangled "horseless carriages." Soon, many could afford one. By the early decades of the twentieth century there were more than two million cars on the road in the United States alone.

Slowly, horses began to disappear from everyday life.

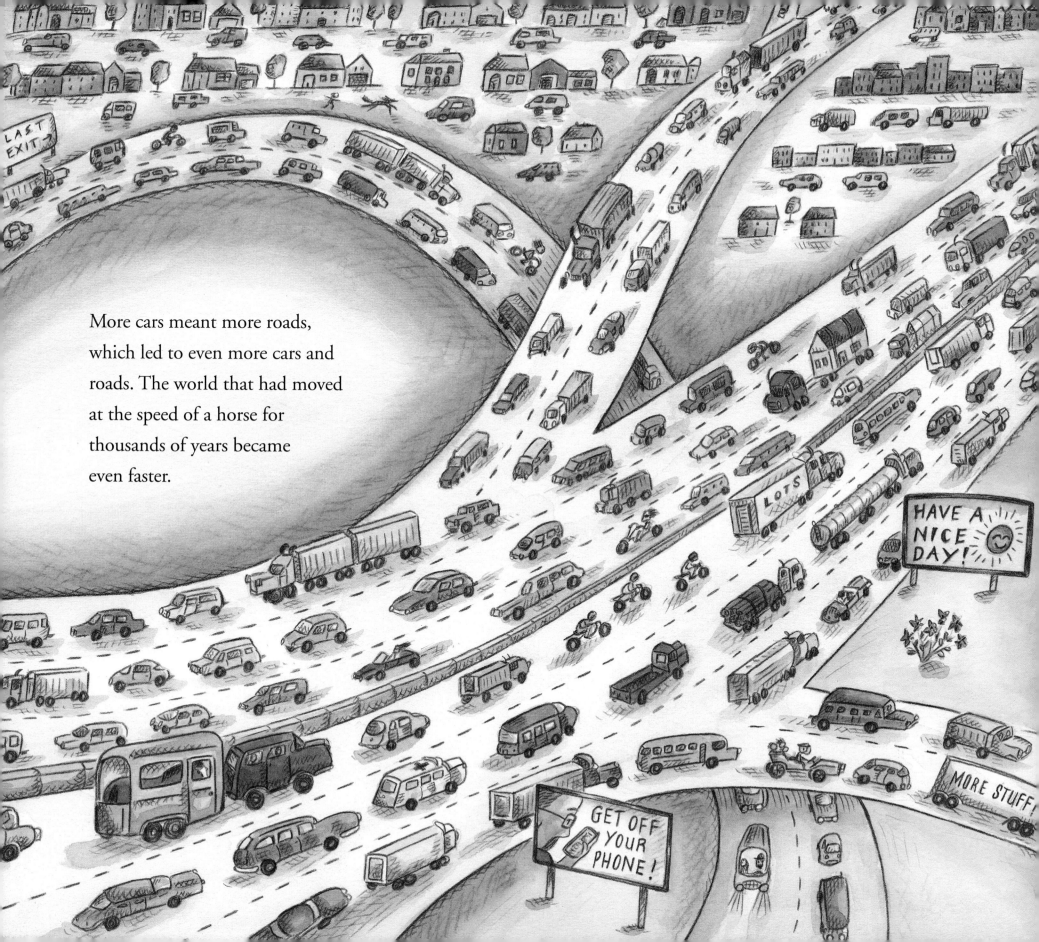

More cars meant more roads, which led to even more cars and roads. The world that had moved at the speed of a horse for thousands of years became even faster.

Humans traded manure in the streets for pollution in the air. More than two billion cars on the planet today burn gas and oil taken from deep underground. Earth's climate—that has changed in slow cycles over billions of years—is now changing rapidly, due in part to so many automobiles.

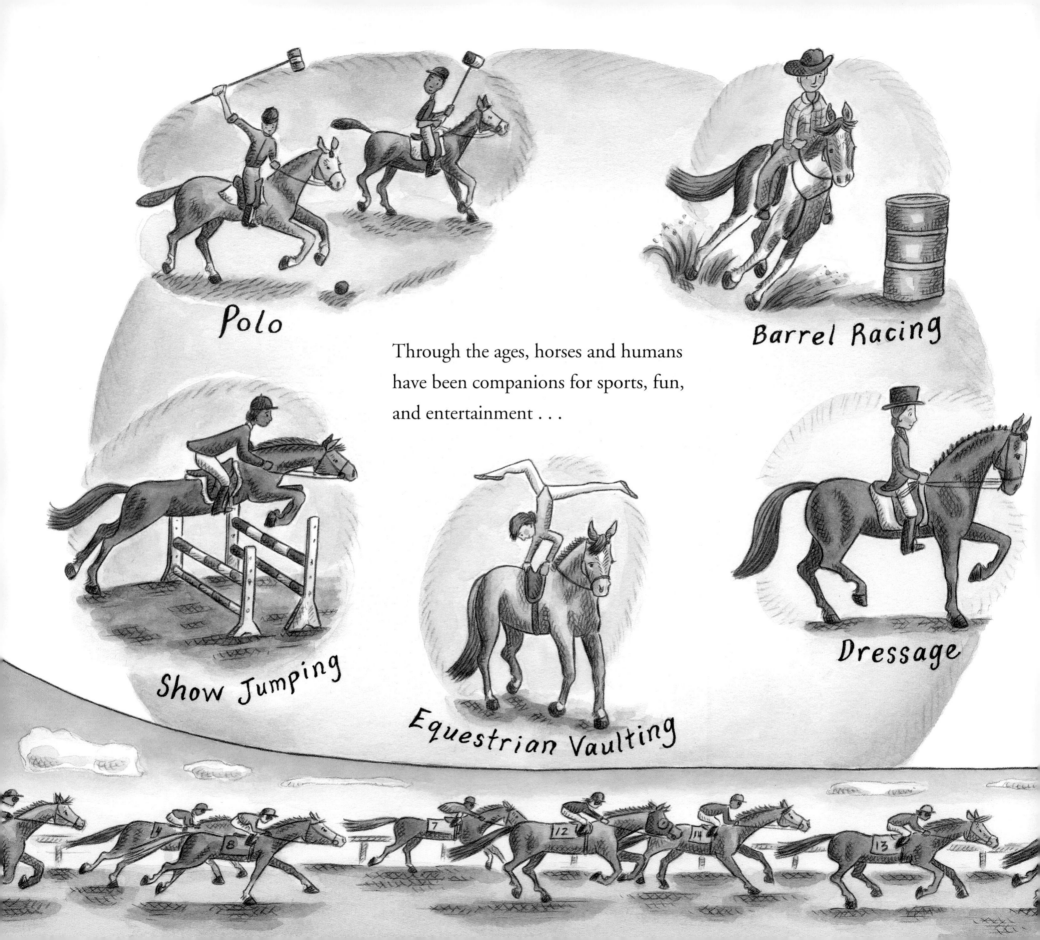

Polo

Barrel Racing

Through the ages, horses and humans have been companions for sports, fun, and entertainment . . .

Show Jumping

Equestrian Vaulting

Dressage

Three-Day Eventing

Steer Roping (Rodeo)

Circus Horses

. . . and though some humans have mistreated them, many more respect and treasure their connection with horses.

Spanish Riding School – Lipizzaner Stallions

Harness Racing

Alberta Mountain horses (Wildies)
CANADA

Dartmoor, Exmoor and New Forest ponies
ENGLAND

Sable Island horses
CANADA

Mustangs
U.S.A.

Chincoteague ponies
U.S.A.

Camargue horses
FRANCE

Sorraia horses
PORTUGAL

Lavradeiro horses
BRAZIL

Patagonia wild horses
CHILE & ARGENTINA

The only *truly* wild horse on earth is Przewalski's horse, because it has never been domesticated by humans. Named for a Russian explorer, the breed nearly became extinct from being hunted and captured for zoo exhibits. Now called the "takhi horse" in Mongolia, the horses have been bred in captivity and rereleased into the wild with help from conservation programs!

Gotland ponies
SWEDEN

Konik horses
POLAND

Yakut horses
SIBERIA, RUSSIA

takhi horses
MONGOLIA

Misaki horses
JAPAN

Delft Island horses
SRI LANKA

Namib Desert Horses
NAMIBIA

Rooisand horses
SOUTH AFRICA

Brumbies
AUSTRALIA

Kaimanawa horses
NEW ZEALAND

Wherever humans brought horses, some always escaped or were set loose.
These feral horses still roam on parts of the planet today.

Horses and humans have lived and worked together for thousands of years. Although horses are not a part of everyday life anymore, humans still wonder at this magnificent animal. The world would be a different place if horses had never existed!

And from atop a horse's back, it will always be a more magical one.

# AUTHOR'S NOTE

For thousands of years, horses were everywhere, every day. Horses have been used around the world for transportation, agriculture, war, and conquest. Horses inspired humans to create art and invent new machines. They enabled humans to colonize lands and expand empires. Horse and human life were intertwined and inseparable, yet the role of the everyday horse throughout history is rarely mentioned.

The horse is embedded in human culture.

"Horse" words and expressions are woven throughout our language. Horsing around, to give free rein to someone, unbridled (enthusiasm), to give someone a leg up, chomping at the bit, hold your horses, the ponytail (hairstyle), and more . . . are all still said today, even by people who have never seen an actual horse!

Horses have been the subject of myth and folklore. They have been worshipped as gods and regarded as emblems of wealth, status, and power. For ages, the horseshoe has been considered a symbol of luck. Some people believe keeping the U shape up holds good luck in, while others believe turning it upside down lets bad luck flow out. (You decide!)

Horses didn't completely disappear when cars came on the scene. They continued to be used into the mid-twentieth century. People in many p: of the world still use horses for farming and ranching—where the terrain can be too rugged for motorized vehicles, and cowhands can trust their horses' instincts to help herd cattle.

People who rely exclusively on the horse for power still exist today, such as the Amish, who use horses and buggies instead of cars, and the Kazak people in Mongolia, who migrate through the seasons on horseback wit their herds of livestock.

As with many animals, horses have not always been treated kindly by humans. The American Society for the Prevention of Cruelty to Animals (ASPCA) was founded in 1866 in New York City in response t: overworked and underfed street horses. Today, rescue organizations help save horses that have been misused and discarded by the horse-racing industry and other sports. It is humans' responsibility to protect the hor

The horse's evolution is complex. Fossil bones show their progression from creatures with toes to the single-hooved animals we know today. Paleontologists study the wear marks on fossilized teeth for clues about what horses ate, when they were first ridden, and what the earth was like

Horses can run so fast that the human eye can't always see how their legs move. In 1879, Eadweard Muybridge used a new stop-motion film technique to photograph the sequence of a horse's gait. He proved that during the gallop, all four hooves are off

...en early horses existed. Scientists are always learning more about the ...ginnings of the horse as new fossils are found.

...eolithic-era cave drawings of horses and other creatures give rise ...questions about the world horses and humans lived in, and why ...mans drew the horse's image. Perhaps they indicate the human need ...record our lives, and make art from our surroundings. Some mysteries ...l probably never be solved. But the drawings illustrate the strong ...nnection that prehistoric humans must have had to the horse.

...rses can be calm, clever, feisty, gentle, amusing, affectionate, and ...al. They each have a unique personality, and can develop close bonds ...h their humans. They are part of our world, yet there is something ...ut the horse that seems as if they live in a world of their own. Perhaps ...s enigma is part of the enduring fascination humans have with horses.

...st humans can name at least one famous horse—whether from the ...vies, a racehorse, a horse from mythology, or a character from a ...orite book. But think about everything that has happened throughout ...tory before the automobile was invented. Once you become aware of ...role horses played in our past, you will see them everywhere!

...rses have changed the course of human history more than any other ...mal in the world. This book is my tribute to the everyday ones that ...erve our respect and gratitude.

# SELECT SOURCES

Chamberlin, J. Edward. *Horse: How the Horse Has Shaped Civilizations*. New York: Blue Bridge, 2006.

Clutton-Brock, Juliet. *Horse Power: A History of the Horse and the Donkey in Human Societies*. Cambridge, MA: Harvard University Press, 1992.

Dent, Anthony Austen. *The Horse Through Fifty Centuries of Civilization*. New York: Holt, Rinehart and Winston, Phaidon Press Limited, 1974.

Dutson, Judith. Photography by Bob Langrish. *Storey's Illustrated Guide to 96 Horse Breeds of North America*. North Adams, MA: Storey, 2005.

Greene, Anne Norton. *Horses at Work: Harnessing Power in Industrial America*. Cambridge, MA: Harvard University Press, 2008.

Hendricks, Bonnie L. *International Encyclopedia of Horse Breeds*. Norman, OK: University of Oklahoma Press, 2007.

Jurmain, Suzanne. *Once Upon a Horse: A History of Horses—and How They Shaped Our History*. New York: Lothrop, Lee & Shepard, 1989.

Muybridge, Eadweard. *Animals in Motion*. Edited by Lewis S. Brown. New York: Dover, 1957.

Olsen, Sandra L., editor. *Horses Through Time*. Boulder, CO: Roberts Rinehart Publishers for Carnegie Museum of Natural History, 1996.

Williams, Wendy. *The Horse: The Epic History of Our Noble Companion*. New York: Scientific American/Farrar, Straus and Giroux, 2015.

the ground at the same time. (For centuries, artists had depicted horses in a "flying gallop"—with legs *incorrectly* extended straight out, front and back!)

# TIMELINE

**56 million years ago**
The first horses, *Eohippus*, or *Hyracotherium* ("dawn horses"), appear on earth. The predecessors of today's modern horse will evolve in North America.

**4 million years ago**
Horses evolve to their modern form, *Equus*.

**2.5 million years ago**
Prehistoric horses exist across Eurasia.

**20,000 years ago**
The Bering Land Bridge connects North America and Asia during the Ice Age.

**11,000 years ago**
Sea levels rise and the Bering Land Bridge is submerged. Horses become extinct in North America.

**11,000–3,000 years ago**
Humans begin to plant crops and to keep domestic animals.

**5,500 years ago**
Horses are domesticated by humans, likely across the Eurasian Steppes and possibly in multiple areas.

**5,500 years ago**
The wheel is invented in Mesopotamia by the ancient Sumerians for use as a potter's wheel.

**2,400 years ago**
King Cyrus the Great of Persia creates the first post delivery system to deliver messages using horses and riders across the Persian Empire. It is later used as a model for post delivery in the Roman Empire and the Mongol Empire under Genghis Khan.

**700 BCE**
The Circus Maximus is built in Rome for chariot racing. The Romans use boots created to protect the horses' hooves, called "hipposandals." Metal horseshoes will be made in later years.

**521–486 BCE**
Polo is first played during the reign of Darius I in ancient Persia (Iran). It later spreads to India and China.

**500 BCE**
Leather toe stirrups are used in India. Iron stirrups are later developed in China.

**430–355 BCE**
The Greek philosopher Xenophon writes his book *The Art of Horsemanship*.

**300 BCE**
The horse collar is invented in China.

**711**
The Moors invade Spain, bringing Barb horses to the Iberian Peninsula.

**847**
Vikings invade Iceland and bring horses to the area.

**1000**
Metal horseshoes, nailed onto a horse's hooves, become widespread in Europe.

**1066**
The Normans use horses to conquer England in the Battle of Hastings, as recorded on the Bayeux Tapestry, which still exists today.

**1095–1492**
European knights use heavy horses in a series of religious wars called the Crusades.

**1206–1368**
The Mongol Empire, founded by Genghis Khan and using thousands of horses, covers nine million square miles across Eurasia.

**1493**
Christopher Columbus brings horses to the island of Hispaniola (Haiti/Dominican Republic).

**1519**
Hernán Cortés invades what is today Mexico, bringing horses to the mainland.

**1521**
Ponce de León brings horses to today's Florida while searching for gold.

**1572**
The Spanish Riding School is founded in Vienna, Austria. The world-famous Lipizzaner horses still perform there today.

**1625**
Friesian horses are brought to New Amsterdam (Manhattan) by the Dutch West India Company.

**1653**
Horses are brought to South Africa by the Dutch East India Company.

**1710**
By now, most Native American nations across North America have horses.

**1750–1850**
As improved roadways are constructed, many different types of wagons, carriages, and wheeled vehicles are built for horses to pull.

**1776**

Scottish inventor James Watt patents an improved steam engine, which will influence the Industrial Revolution.

**1788**

The English bring horses to Botany Bay, Australia.

**1791**

The *General Stud Book*, the first official Thoroughbred horse registry, is established in England.

**1825**

The Stockton and Darlington Railway opens in England. It is the first passenger steam locomotive.

**1828–1835**

Inventors develop early electric cars in the Netherlands, Hungary, and the United States, but they are not practical to drive.

**1842**

The Mines and Colleries Act 1842 forbids women, girls, and boys younger than ten years old from working in British coal mines. However, horses and ponies are still allowed.

**1860–1862**

The Pony Express carries mail between Missouri and California in the U.S.A.

**1866**

The American Society for the Prevention of Cruelty to Animals (ASPCA) is founded in New York City in response to the poor treatment of street horses. It is modeled on the Royal Society for the Prevention of Cruelty to Animals, created in England in 1824.

**1872**

An outbreak of equine influenza, called the Great Epizootic of 1872, paralyzes North American cities because so many horses fall ill.

**1881**

Wild horses are "discovered" in Central Asia by Russian explorer Colonel Nikolai Przewalski, for whom the horses are named.

**1885**

In Germany, Karl Benz invents one of the first gasoline-powered automobiles.

**1890**

Native Americans are killed by the U.S. Army in the Wounded Knee Massacre, in South Dakota. It is one of the final battles of the Indian Wars, fought for nearly three hundred years as Europeans colonized the North American continent. Countless horses belonging to Native Americans are killed in the process.

**1890s**

Practical electric cars are produced and gain in popularity. By the early 1900s, one-third of all cars in the United States are electric.

**Early 1900s**

Horses are used in several expeditions to explore Antarctica.

**1913**

The Ford Motor Company introduces the Model T. The "Tin Lizzie" is the first mass-produced, affordable car.

**1914–1919**

World War I sees the last widespread use of horses in a major war. Around eight million horses lose their lives.

**1922**

The last fire-engine horses are retired in New York City.

**1927**

By now, the Ford Motor Company has produced fifteen million automobiles. Cities throughout the United States are experiencing problems with smog.

**1930s**

Librarians on horseback deliver books to residents of rural Kentucky as part of a New Deal program to improve literacy during the Great Depression.

**1940**

The Lascaux Cave is discovered in France, with prehistoric cave paintings of horses and other animals.

**1970s**

There is renewed interest in using horses for farming due to the energy crisis and the growing environmental movement.

**1971**

Miocene-era fossils from approximately twelve million years ago are discovered on a Nebraska farm. The Ashfall Fossil Beds State Historical Park is designated a National Historic Landmark in 2006.

**1994**

The Chauvet–Pont d'Arc Cave is discovered in France.

**2019**

A well-preserved 42,000-year-old foal from the Pleistocene Epoch is discovered in the melting permafrost in Siberia, Russia.

**2020**

There are more than two billion cars and trucks on earth.

*For Bert,*
*one of my favorites*

The art for this book was created with pencil, watercolor, ink,
and colored pencils on Saunders Waterford watercolor paper.

**Note: As long as thirty thousand years ago, when early humans roamed throughout Europe and Asia and hunted
the horse for food, they painted pictures of horses and other animals on cave walls in places like Lascaux and
the Chauvet–Pont d'Arc Cave in France, and the Cave of Altamira in Spain. The animals were created with charcoal
and mineral pigments mixed with clay or animal fat. Humans also added images of their own hands!**

Library of Congress Cataloging-in-Publication Data:

Names: Thermes, Jennifer, author.
Title: Horse power : how horses changed the world / Jennifer Thermes. Description: New York, NY :
Abrams Books for Young Readers, 2021. | Includes bibliographical references. | Audience: Ages 8 to 12 | Summary:
"Until the popularization of the family car, horses and humans lived, worked, and played side by side. With the invention of the wheel, saddle, bit, and bridle; horses pulled
far-flung lands closer together at the speed of a gallop. Trade, agriculture, exploration, and war—none of these would have been possible in the same way without horses. In dazzling spreads
packed with maps, sidebars, and other hidden gems, Jennifer Thermes tackles the history of the horse. Horse Power explores horses' evolution. It tracks their migration as they find homes on six continents,
and it shows readers what kinds of jobs they've had. And, ultimately, it explores the shift from "horse power" to "horsepower"—when humans traded manure in the street for pollution
in the air. An encyclopedic look this amazing animal, Horse Power offers a unique view of world history from atop a horse's back"—Provided by publisher.
Identifiers: LCCN 2020018550 | ISBN 9781419749452 (hardcover)  Subjects: LCSH: Horses—History—Juvenile literature. | Human-animal
relationships—Juvenile literature. | Animals and civilization—Juvenile literature.
Classification: LCC SF302 .T44 2021 | DDC 636.1—dc23
LC record available at https://lccn.loc.gov/2020018550

Text and illustrations copyright © 2021 Jennifer Thermes
Book design by Pamela Notarantonio

Printed and bound in Thailand
10 9 8 7 6 5 4 3 2

Abrams Books for Young Readers are available at special discounts when purchased in quantity for premiums and promotions as well as fundraising
or educational use. Special editions can also be created to specification. For details, contact specialsales@abramsbooks.com or the address below.

Abrams® is a registered trademark of Harry N. Abrams, Inc.

**ABRAMS** The Art of Books
195 Broadway, New York, NY 10007
abramsbooks.com